D1201723

Read and Play
Trucks

by Jim Pipe

Stargazer Books

truck

2

This is a **truck**.

It carries a heavy load.

3

driver

4

A truck has a **driver**.

The **driver** sits in the cab.

5

wheels

A truck has **wheels**.

Wheels help a truck move.

engine

8

A truck has an **engine**.

The **engine** makes it strong.

9

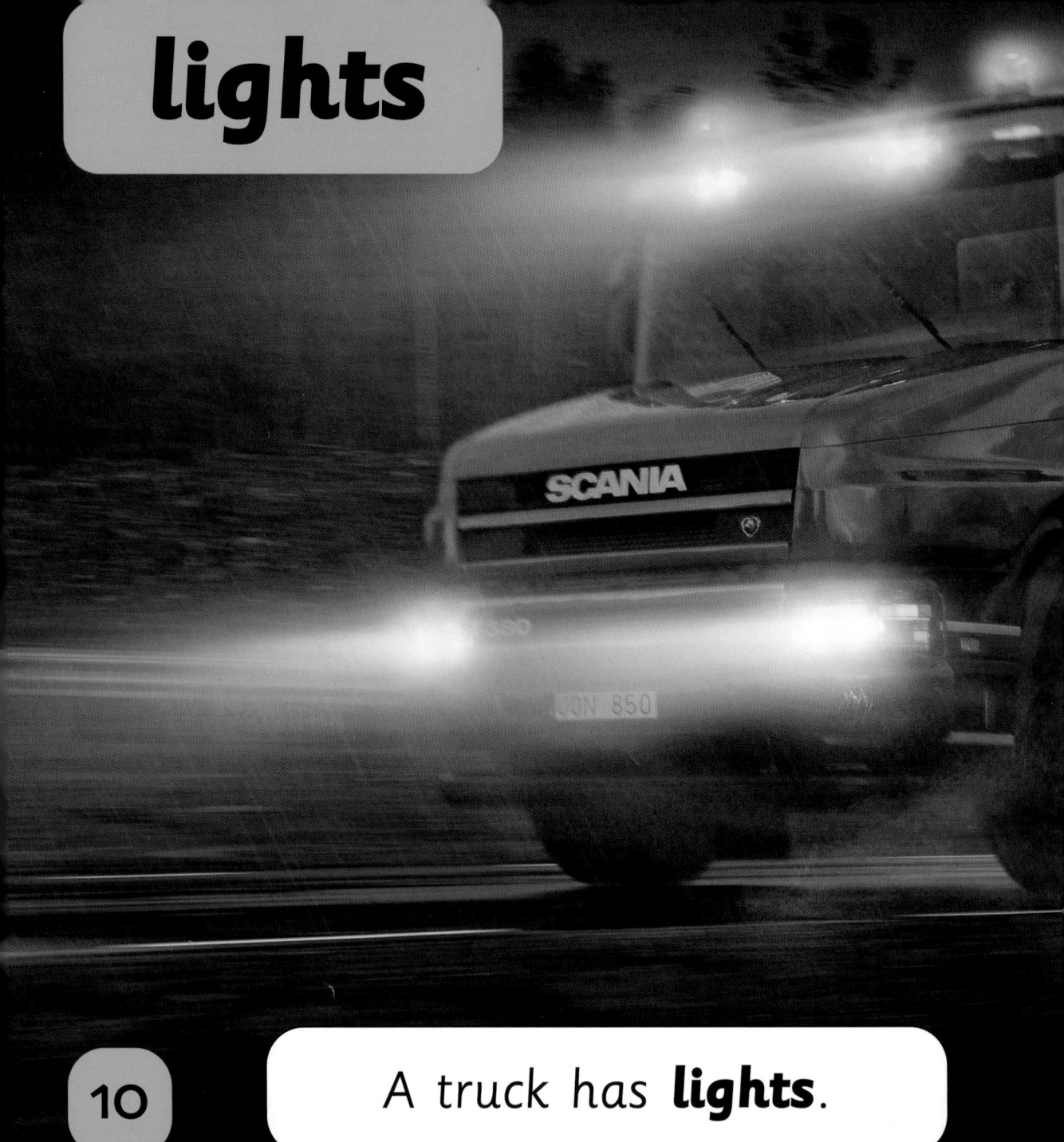

lights

A truck has **lights**.

Lights shine on the road.

11

small

12

This is a **small** truck.

big

This is a very **big** truck.

13

dump

14

This is a **dump** truck.

It **dumps** its load.

15

fire

A **fire** engine puts out **fires**.

16

This truck clears **snow**.

snow

17

slow

18 This giant truck is very **slow**.

fast

This truck is very **fast**.

What am I?

lights

driver

wheel

cab

20

Match the words and pictures.

How many?

Can you count the trucks?

21

What do I do?

What jobs do these trucks do?

Index

Can you find these truck pictures in the book?

23

For Parents and Teachers

Questions you could ask:

p. 2 What color is the truck? e.g. red/silver. Point out shiny parts, black tires, windows, etc, and discuss what materials they are made from.

p. 6 How many wheels can you see? Compare with the number of wheels on other trucks. Remember there are wheels on both sides of truck!

p. 9 What is this truck carrying? e.g. logs. Compare with other loads, e.g. digger, goods, soil, etc.

p. 10 When does a driver turn on the lights? e.g. at night. You could also ask what color the lights are at the back of a truck, e.g. red/yellow.

p. 13 How big is this truck? Point out the man at the front and ask the reader to guess the height, e.g. the truck is as tall as three people.

p. 15 What sound does a truck's horn make? Point out the two horns on top of the cab.

p. 17 Where does the water come from? The fire engine carries the water to the fire. Point out the long hose connected to the fire engine.

p. 18 What is the giant truck carrying? e.g. space shuttle/rocket. The truck moves very slowly as the rocket is very heavy. For scale, note the tiny figure walking alongside the transporter.

Activities you could do:

• Ask the reader to act out driving in a truck, e.g. starting the engine, turning steering wheel, blowing horn, braking, making suitable noises!

• When they are out and about, e.g. on a car journey, ask the reader to spot different kinds of trucks and the jobs that they do.

• Look at how wheels work indoors and outdoors, e.g. on bikes, carts, strollers, and toy cars.

• Encourage the reader to sing action rhymes such as "The Wheels on the Bus."

• Use recycled materials to create models of trucks, e.g. fire engine, dump truck. Include circular items such as foil dishes and plastic lids for wheels.

© Aladdin Books Ltd 2007

Designed and produced by Aladdin Books Ltd

All Rights Reserved

Printed in the United States

Series consultant Zoe Stillwell is an experienced preschool teacher.

First published in 2007 in the United States by Stargazer Books c/o The Creative Company 123 South Broad Street P.O. Box 227 Mankato, Minnesota 56002

Photocredits: *l-left, r-right, b-bottom, t-top, c-center, m-middle* 1, 4, 6-7, 8, 10-11, 16, 17, 20tr & tl, 21, 22tr—Scania. 2-3, 14-15—photos courtesy of Mack Trucks, Inc. 5, 12, 13, 20br & bl, 22b—istockfoto.com. 9—Corbis. 18—NASA. 19—US Navy. 22tr—Photodisc.

Library of Congress Cataloging-in-Publication Data

Pipe, Jim, 1966-
　　Trucks / by Jim Pipe.
　　　　p. cm. -- (Read and play)
　　Includes Index.
　　ISBN 978-1-59604-117-2
　　　1. Trucks--Juvenile literature.
I. Title.

TL230.15.P57 2006
629.224--dc22

2005055532

WITHDRAWN

JUN 03 2021

By: VRW